Sister
Dottie S. Dixon

# The Mormon Kama Sutra

## by Cami Sue Truman

### revised and updated by
## Sister Dottie S. Dixon

## all new illustrations by Pat Bagley

*The Mormon Kama Sutra*

Printed in Utah.

Editor: Dan Thomas

First Edition
9   8   7   6   5   4   3   2   1


ISBN 978-0-9801406-7-5


White Horse Books
1347 S. Glenmare St.
Salt Lake City, Utah 84105
801-556-4615
www.whitehorsebooks.net

# The Mormon Kama Sutra

Good lovin' perduces amazin' results.
For Donnie P. Dixon,
the second love of my life.

—Sister Dottie S. Dixon

## With special thanks to our sex experts who consulted on this project:

Lauren Ball, Kent Frogley, Charles Lynn Frost, Barb Gandy, Randy Lindstrom, Michael Mason, Laurie Mecham, Josh Moon, David Newkirk, Drew Sanders, Fran Pruyn, Leigh Stevens, Tad Telford, Dan Thomas, Troy Williams, Christopher Wixom

# Foreword by Sister Dottie S. Dixon to the 2010 Revised and Updated 40th Anniversary Edition of Cami Sue Truman's "The Mormon Kama Sutra"

Lawsie and Lands Almighty! How excited am I to be presentin' to you this wonderful re-publication of The Marmon Karma Sutress. How many times have I fingered my original copy by the inspired Cami Sue Truman? How many times have I dog-eared my favert positions so me and my hubby, Don, can revisit them over and over and over again? How many copies did I buy fer friends who seemed to need that little bit-o-spice back in their marital lives? I have the strongest testimony that this book can save, reboot, and even launch a marriage. It's fer the beginner (virgin), the mid-sized (somebody wantin' to experiment a bit), and the ultimative perfessional in all things sextual.

And then to have the good Lard send that ever-so-handsome and talented Pat Bagley into yer life! We met years ago at a wedding fer my cousin Penny Pennypacker, who married a rich insurance salesman upta Salt Lake City. I was completely enamerated by his talent way back then—but to think I've finally gotten the opportunity to collabrate with him on this new edition of The Marmon Karma Sutress. He is soo handsome and creative, and quietly mysterious—sarta like that Harrison Fard in that movie, Invaders of the Last Arc. He has gone and created the best illustrations anyone could ever hope fer. It was a creative match guided from above, I'm just sayin'!

You can't tell me the angels don't hover over Sister Dottie and guide her when, where and to who she needs to go. And they told me this book needs to be shared with a whole new generation of Saints who need to know the ins and outs and inbetweens of sexual relations. So Pat Bagley and I enhanced Sister Cami Sue's brilliant original with some extra-special sections of our own. And I've added my very own blow-by-blow commentary ta make sure ya understand it all. And I can't write another word without thanking my scribes for this here new translation, Troy Williams and that strange friend 'a his, Charles Lynn Frost.

Oh, I'll never ferget my honeymoon downta romantic Panguitch, Utah, thirty-plus years ago. On that cold winter's night in the tiny Zion Motor Lodge, I was ever so nervous . . . and a total virgin! My younger sister, Wendy, the charcoal sheep of our family, was never so inspired than when she give this here book to my honey, Don, just befare our honeymoon clear back in 1973. Don, my very own E.C., er, Eternal Companion, is the first love of my life. Sister Cami Sue's book filled those very words, Eternal Companion, with the greatest of meaning.

Don and me have tried each and every position in this here book, and let me tell ya, it has kept our sex life perkier than a chihuahua's little tail. I whole-heartedly endarse this book packed plum full of everything ya need to make yer sex life ever so much more fun. Sex is not naughty, dirty, er something to be ashamed of, but adult play, and should be seen that way.

My admitted favert position in this book, "The Y Mount," perduced Donnie P. Dixon, the second love of my life, and our only child. Now you show me a book that can guarantee somethin' that wonderful!

Oh, oh, oh, one more thing: my gay son Donnie reminded me—Mom, it's the 21st century, ya gotta have pictures and positions in here of people who look differnt than you and Dad. Well, heck, I thought to maself, he's right. Ya gotta be more inclushal, Dottie. And so we've gone and taken inta consideration all types of humans and their sexual needs and desires. So fer the Gays and Lesbitarians out there, yer all a part of this new and improved book, too. Celebrate yerselves!

Because of this book, I'm no longer that dumbed-out little girl I usta be, sex-wise. Thank heavens fer that! So take a letter, Maria, address it to my wife, say I've gone and bought the new Marmon Karma Sutress, we're gonna spark our sex life!

Amen and amen!

-Sister Dottie S. Dixon
Spanish Fork, Utah
September 2009

# Foreword by Cami Sue Truman to the 1970 edition of "The Mormon Kama Sutra"

**Y**ou hold in your hands the fulfillment of a heavenly promise. In the last days, a mighty work would come forth to deliver the Saints from the perverts, deviants and unspeakable sexual abominations that have been running rampant in the world.

The Mormon Kama Sutra was discovered in 1890 by the forgotten Mormon archeologist Hector Faust Norlander—my great grandfather. While traveling in South America, he discovered an ancient papyrus from Mayan (i.e., Lamanite) ruins. He brought his findings to a harried Church President, Wilford Woodruff, who pleaded, "Look, Hec, get back to me when this whole polygamy thing blows over. We'll talk then." (The Lost Writings of Hector F. Norlander, p. 1,362)

It never came to pass. Norlander was killed in a bison stampede while excavating an especially lucrative Anasazi burial site. The ancient papyrus was lost to the world yet again.

In 1967, as an unwed virginal daughter of perpetual promise from La Verkin, Utah, I knew a special calling awaited me. And verily, one August afternoon the sun was hot, and the young men worked in the orchard on the banks of the Virgin River. They were digging and hoeing, their sinews wet with the sweat of the simmering summer sun—and it was there that I received an intense prompting that pierced deep within me. I was impressed upon to return home and take a cold shower. Then I noticed the boxes stuffed back in the towel drawer. There I discovered the ancient papyrus.

That night in my dreams, I received a visitation from Great Grandfather Norlander. He told me there was great sexual confusion in the land. Many of the Saints were being led astray by Betty Friedan, Tiny Tim, and the perky blond twins from Kanab featured in last July's Playboy. "The devil's work!" Great Grandad thundered. He continued by explaining how the Indians (Oriental, not Nephite) had perverted the original texts of the Kama Sutra with their sexually licentious false animal gods. I was told that I would be given the gift of translation to reveal the one true original Kama Sutra (Nephite, not Oriental).

But I doubted. How could a virgin such as I, so unacquainted with men and things, possibly reveal this work? Grandfather assured me that this is exactly how all heavenly books are revealed—through a pure vessel, unsullied by worldly experience or academic credentials.

And sure enough, that night I started writing—grasping the pen all day and all night, not even ceasing to sleep! I couldn't stop. I wrote and wrote and wrote, refusing to sheath my writing utensil! I wrote more and more, until lo, many great and burning sensations came bursting from my bosoms! And today, you hold in your hands this inspired translation.

The scriptural commandment to "bridle one's passions" doesn't mean you have to shoot the horse. You first have to learn to manage the horse. Then you only have to point your body, parts and passions in the proper direction, snap the reins, and before you know it, you and your Eternal Companion (E.C.) are trotting down the road to eternal happiness and worlds without end!

Now go forth to multiply and plenish!

-Cami Sue Truman
La Verkin, Utah
April 1970

*A note to those Mayan scholars who are "wise with the teachings of men" and claim the papyrus is a lunar agricultural calendar; just pay them no heed!

# Foreword by the Illustrator to the Sister Dottie S. Dixon 2010 Revised and Updated 40th Anniversary Edition of Cami Sue Truman's "The Mormon Kama Sutra"

**W**hile Cami Sue Truman's 1970 "The Mormon Kama Sutra" is certainly groundbreaking, it is also a graphic mess. Truman chose to illustrate her inspired work with clippings, hacked up and frankensteined together, from *Ladies Home Journal* and ads from *The Deseret News*. While conveying the general idea, her coital collages were hampered by clothing them in BYU-approved swimwear—the sexiest thing then sanctioned by the LDS Church. (see figure 1). One is left with the general impression of endlessly creative dry humping.

*fig 1. a couple in the throes of missionary position passion.*

When the redoubtable Dottie S. Dixon first approached me to update the "MoKama," as it is known in literary circles, I begged off, knowing myself inadequate to the task. But Sister Dottie's unflagging, patient faith in me and persistence finally inspired me to take a stab at it.

First, I had to see the Norlander papers. I was appalled to discover they were being used as Diet Coke (smuggled in, as it happens) coasters by the staff at the LDS Church History Library. After rescuing the soggy fragments, I painstakingly pieced them together and was rewarded by not only Norlander's facsimiles of the Nephite drawings (see figure 2), but also Cami Sue Truman's original notes in the margins!

*fig 2. Depicts either mesoamerican coitus, or, the banana squash goddess Xenochiccatlcantucl in furious eternal combat with the layabout trickster, Cautlaholchuacahnixtl.*

From these and other sources, I have reconstructed what Cami Sue claimed to have heard from her great grandfather Norlander in a dream about his interpretation of the papers he discovered in Latin America more than a century ago. I have updated the illustrations and taken the daring leap of depicitng the male and female figures unabashedly, unashamedly, and unappealingly, naked.

-Pat Bagley
Salt Lake City, Utah
September 2009

# Glossary

Down There — Anything south of the belt and north of the knees

Privates — See "down there"

Loins — See "privates"

Penis — The male member

Subpoena — Just below the male member

Breastiality — An unhealthy fascination with bosoms

Bosoms — The brestial part of a female

Ohmyheck spot — Down there somewhere

Seed — Can be mail-ordered from Burpees in the spring

Knowing — King James English for "knocked up"

# Glossary (cont.)

| | | |
|---|---|---|
| Heavy Petting | — | . . . is grrrrrrrrrreat! |
| Eternal Companion | — | (also E.C.) the only person you're ever going to have sex with . . . ever |
| Gay | — | Happy, fun-loving, good with hair and show tunes |
| Sodomite | — | Person who installs lawns |
| Dry Hump | — | Arid Provo hillock on which BYU singles housing is built |
| Brokeback Mormon | — | Gay men who marry straight women at behest of their bishop |
| Active Member | — | Gets some twice a week |
| Less-active member | — | Might get lucky on birthday and anniversary |
| Non-member | — | Males surprised to find themselves resurrected in the Telestial Kingdom resembling a Ken doll |

Your Body
is a
Temple

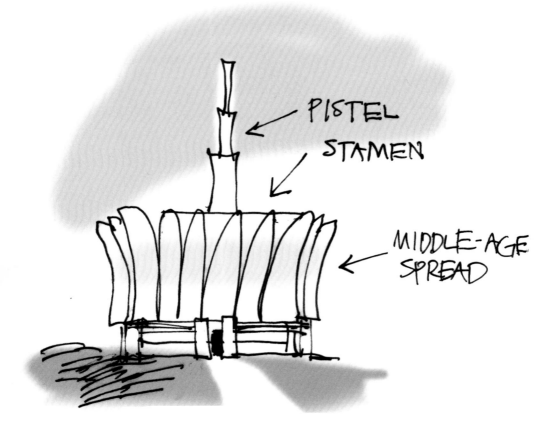

PISTEL

STAMEN

MIDDLE-AGE
SPREAD

*It stands ta reason that if the body is a temple, then temples are also kinda like a body, with signs like "No Parking" and "Keep Off the Grass."*

# Temple/Body Erroneous Zones

# The Male Organ

*Crimanentlee!*

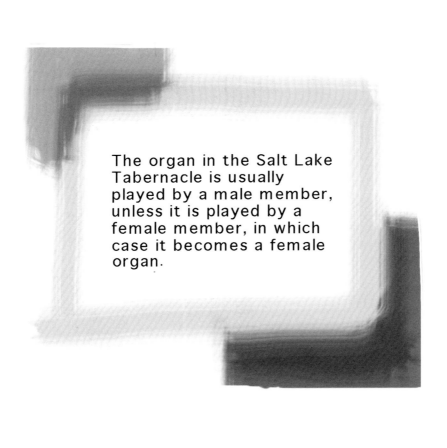

The organ in the Salt Lake Tabernacle is usually played by a male member, unless it is played by a female member, in which case it becomes a female organ.

*Don't get caught kissin' by the organ or ya could get arrested and written up in some gentile newspaper.*

# the Oh! My! Heck! Spot

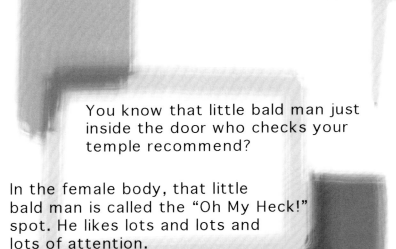

You know that little bald man just inside the door who checks your temple recommend?

In the female body, that little bald man is called the "Oh My Heck!" spot. He likes lots and lots and lots of attention.

 *This little guy is tickled pink when ya find him!*

# Latter-day Foreplay

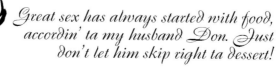

*Great sex has always started with food, accordin' ta my husband Don. Just don't let him skip right ta dessert!*

The whole priesthood-authority thing is pretty good on paper, but if you ever want to play "Hide the Rameumptom" with your E.C., soft-pedal the line about how you are infallible in your sphere of influence.

*Remember who wears the pants,*
*even if you're not wearing any!*

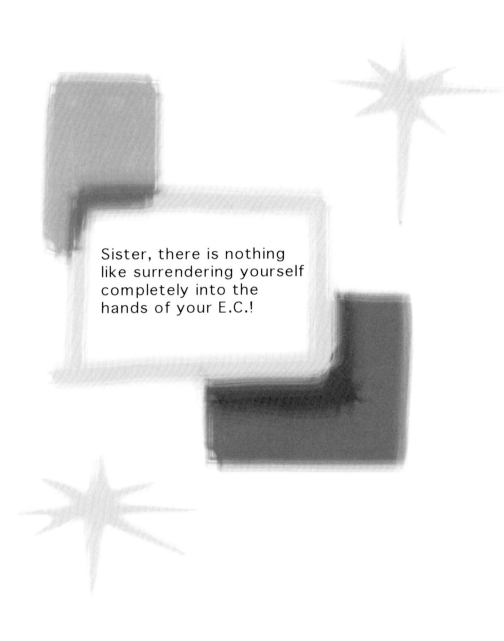

Sister, there is nothing like surrendering yourself completely into the hands of your E.C.!

# Mountain Meadows Massage

*Don and me have one of them nifty heavy duty hand-held massagers at home. Be careful: on High, it'll take off skin, on Low, it'll put yer partner ta sleep.*

Be open with your
E.C. about your
wants and desires.

# Confessin' Your Whims

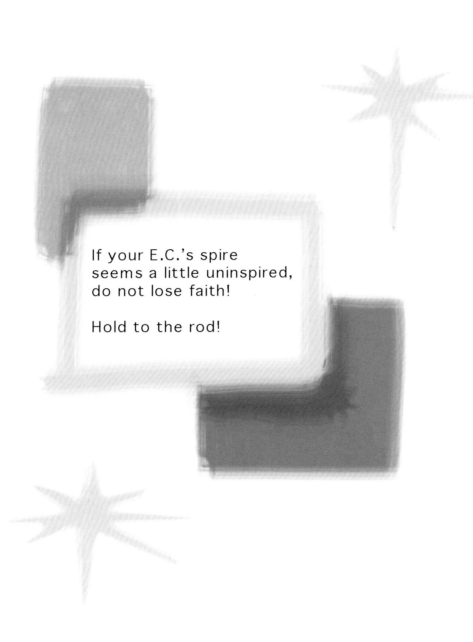

If your E.C.'s spire
seems a little uninspired,
do not lose faith!

Hold to the rod!

# The Salamander Handler

*Trust me, with age, this becomes less icky . . . and much smaller.*

This would be an ideal place
to discuss garments.

As if.

# Naughty Underwear

A FRILLY LITTLE NUMBER CAN BE VERY ALLURING

TIGHTY-WHITEYS, NOT SO MUCH

*My dear sister Wendy is the master at this. Thank Heaven's she introduced me to Victoria's big ole secret.*

# Fantasy Home Evening

Let's try some role playing!
Your E.C. can pretend to be a 19th century
polygamist who's just been with his 16th wife
and is now coming to be with you, his 17th!

Greet him at the door wearing
nothing but an iron skillet.

# Big Love

*Don Dixon! If you read this page,
don't even be thinkin' 'bout it, mister!*

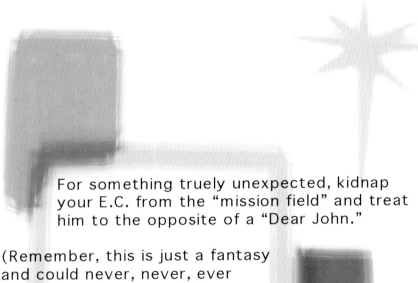

For something truely unexpected, kidnap your E.C. from the "mission field" and treat him to the opposite of a "Dear John."

(Remember, this is just a fantasy and could never, never, ever happen in the real world).

# Mission Improbable

*If yer gonna kidnap the missionary of yer dreams, always make sure it's consenshul!*

Remember how "Titanic" inspired a video store in Orem to create "clean" versions of racy films?

In the sanctity of marriage, you and your E.C. get to be un-cut, uncensored . . .

. . . totally "R!"

# TIT ANIC

The bishop said the reason the Titanic sank was because of people promiscuosly posing naked! I got my doubts about that.

# Authorized & Correlated Positions

Give your E.C. a firm handshake
while making direct eye contact
to convey your sincerity.

# Missionary Position

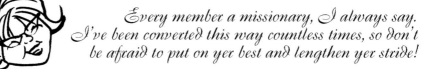

*Every member a missionary, I always say.*
*I've been converted this way countless times, so don't*
*be afraid to put on yer best and lengthen yer stride!*

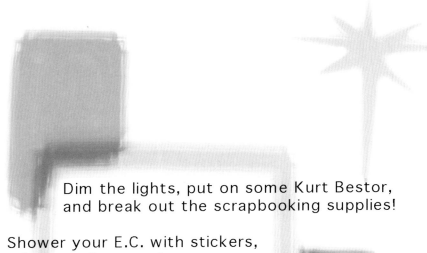

Dim the lights, put on some Kurt Bestor,
and break out the scrapbooking supplies!

Shower your E.C. with stickers,
rub-ons, glitter and . . .

make some memories!

# The Scrapbooker

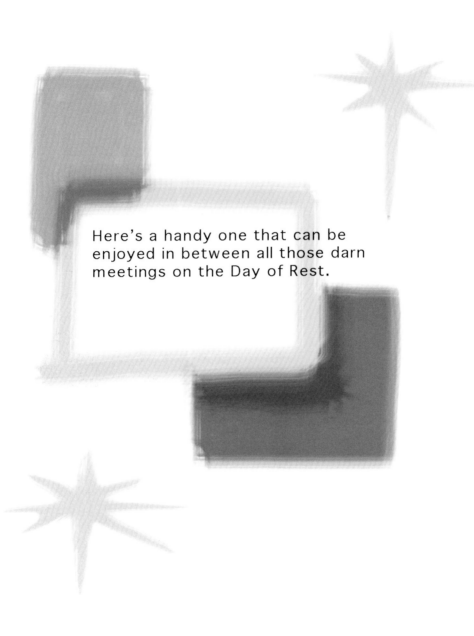

Here's a handy one that can be enjoyed in between all those darn meetings on the Day of Rest.

# Fast Sunday

*Be careful: you don't wanna get
distracted and burn yer pot roast.*

LDS couples love
playing games!

# Twister

*A wholesome Family Home Evening game at the BY gets a bit more frisky once yer lawfully wedded to your E.C.*

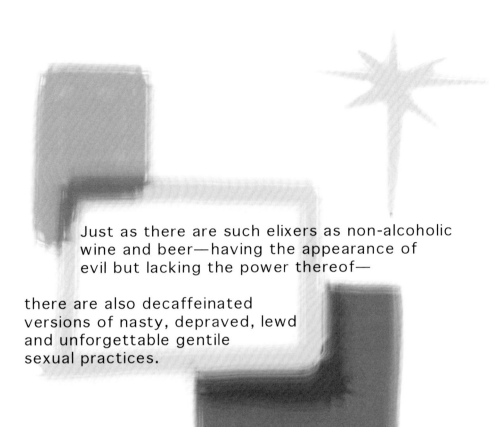

Just as there are such elixers as non-alcoholic
wine and beer—having the appearance of
evil but lacking the power thereof—

there are also decaffeinated
versions of nasty, depraved, lewd
and unforgettable gentile
sexual practices.

# Mile High Club

BRRRRARRRRp.

*Just as in life, the real danger is during take-off and landing.*

Your E.C. may try to mask her interest
in sexual congress by feigning death.

# Work for the Dead

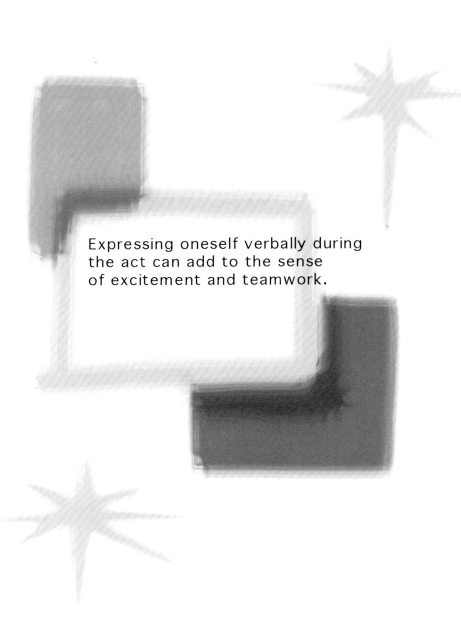

Expressing oneself verbally during the act can add to the sense of excitement and teamwork.

# Rise and Shout

*Sometimes I get so carried away
I start ta do that wave thing.*

The minivan was a revelation given by God in these latter-days to Lee Iacocca to accomodate all those billions of spirits waiting for a body in the pre-existence.

On a related note, sometimes the only thing between you and all those billions of spirits is a bit of latex.

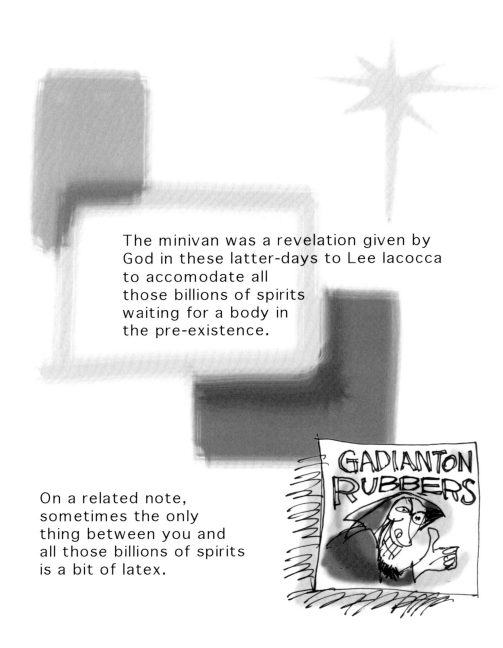

GADIANTON RUBBERS

# Put Your Shoulder to the Wheel

The reason you do it . . .

. . . is because it's there!

# The "Y" Mount

*This very position perduced our Donnie... on our honeymoon, no less. A miracle position!*

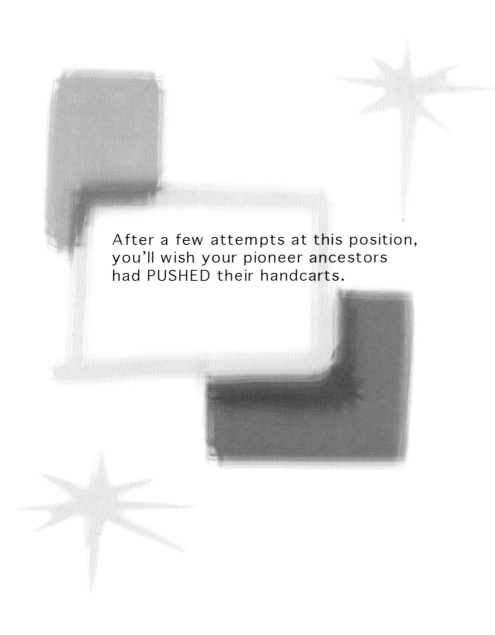

After a few attempts at this position, you'll wish your pioneer ancestors had PUSHED their handcarts.

# Pulling the Handcart

If there's two things us Mormons are good at, it's historical handcart reenactments and marital reproduction. So why not put the two together? Pioneer costumes a plus!

It's perfectly acceptable to revisit something that was so gosh darn exciting from your past.

# The Jell-O Pin

*K-Y Jell-O comes in lime, strawberry and banana! Mmmm . . . my favert!*

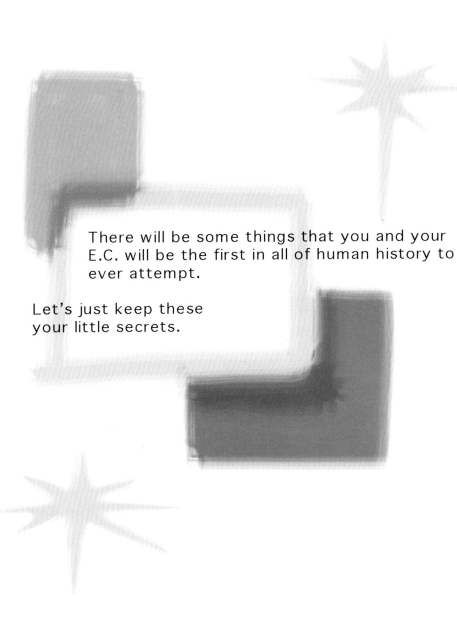

There will be some things that you and your E.C. will be the first in all of human history to ever attempt.

Let's just keep these your little secrets.

# Secret Combinations

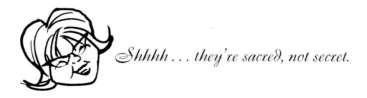

*Shhhh . . . they're sacred, not secret.*

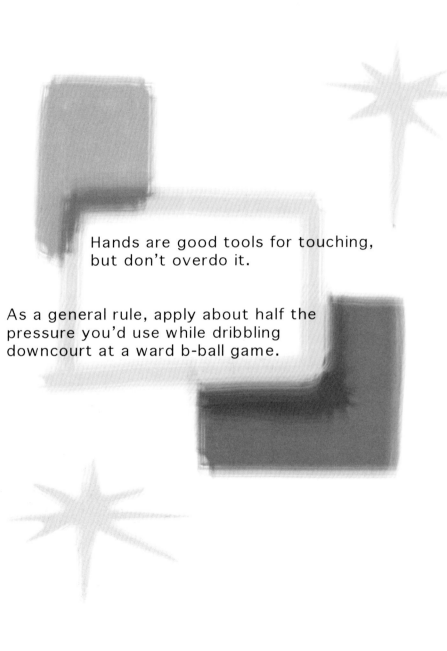

Hands are good tools for touching, but don't overdo it.

As a general rule, apply about half the pressure you'd use while dribbling downcourt at a ward b-ball game.

# Laying on of Hands

Lay off nagging about your E.C. gaining weight or you may find yourself doing a position called the "Eight Cow Wife."

# Seagull and the Cricket

Good Mormons don't let unwholesome
thoughts sully the spirit before marriage.
A virginal mind in a virginal body,
I always say.

However, purity leads to confusion
if newlyweds don't know where to slip
the fast offering envelope,
in a manner of speaking.

It may fall to the new bride to
direct her E.C.'s little pioneer
to the promised land.

# This is the Place

It may come as a revelation to some brethren that women feel sexual, too.

# The Burning Bush

 *Now, I'm no expert, but I'm told if you keep the law of chastity and only ever have sexual relations with yer E.C., this should NOT be a problem!*

# Other Kindsa Sextuality

*As promised,
here's the new sectional.*

Before the '70s, there was no such thing as a "Gay Mormon."

Then two R.M.s, Lance and Todd, broke into the Lamanite costume locker at the Mormon Miracle Pageant.

Once they came out of Pandora's Closet, Lance and Todd were looking FABULOUS, and there was no way to get the gay toothpaste back into the LDS "heteros-only" tube.

# Flaming Cherubim

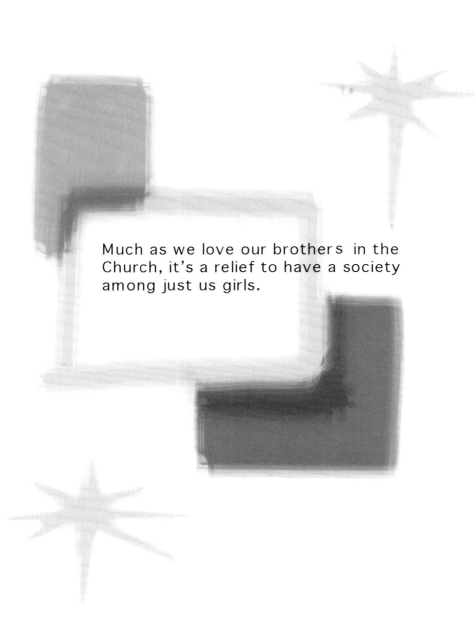

Much as we love our brothers in the Church, it's a relief to have a society among just us girls.

# The Sister-wives Club

You and two friends
get zipped.

# Triple Combination

*I'm sure one of 'em is there to chaperone.*

Sex aversion therapy at BYU in the 70s backfired when it was voted "Kinkiest New Kick" by subscribers to *The Sadomasochist's Friend*.

# LDS & M

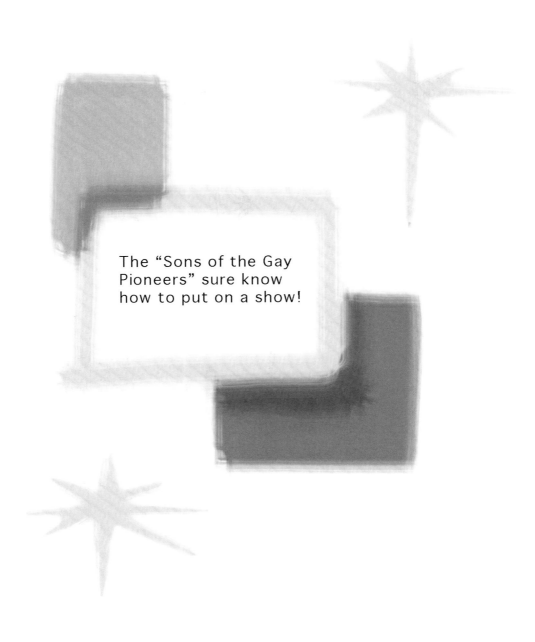

The "Sons of the Gay Pioneers" sure know how to put on a show!

# Stripping Warriors

The Bible tells the story of Onan,
who "spilled" his seed on the ground,
for which God killed him.

The lesson here is obvious—
work on your coordination.

# I Have Two Little Hands
## (and a high-speed modem)

*Eeeew! Fer icky!*